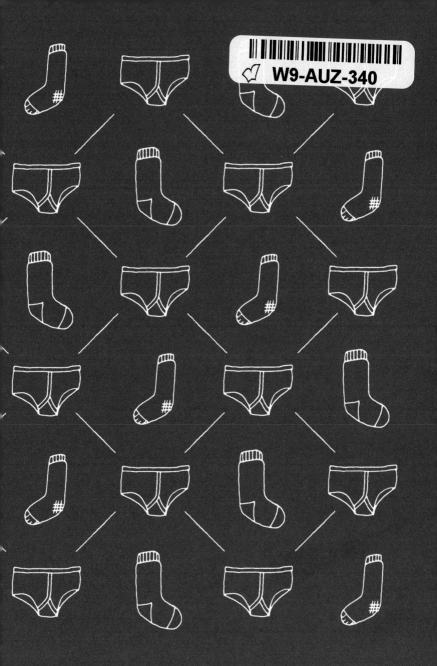

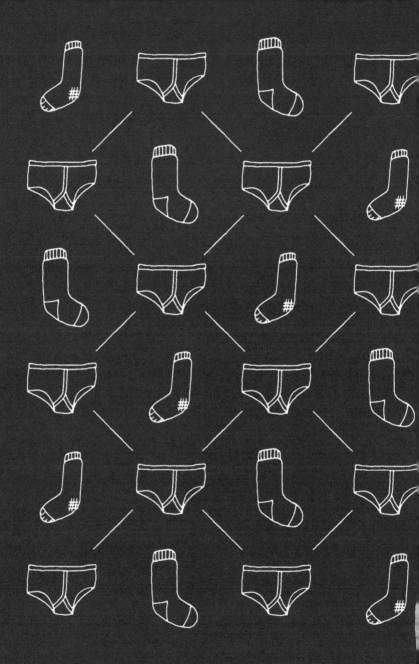

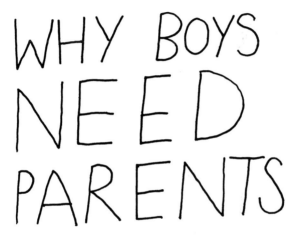

WHY BOYS NEED PARENTS

Alex Beckerman

CHRONICLE BOOKS

SAN FRANCISCO

Library of Congress Cataloging-in-
Publication Data available.

ISBN: 978-1-4521-4734-5

Manufactured in China

Designed by Ben Kither
Picture Editor, Julien Tomasello

Chronicle Books LLC
680 Second Street,
San Francisco, California, 94107
www.chroniclebooks.com

10 9 8 7 6 5 4 3 2 1

Dedicated to boys everywhere, young and old.

Introduction.

The invention of fire occurred when Ogg Jr. decided to see what happens when you rub rocks together near the sulfur pit. Fire was born.

This led immediately to the invention of the time-out.

Boys will be boys. Unfortunately, they will also be arsonists, wrecking balls, flooders, and eight-limbed ninjas of destruction. It is their nature. Boys are driven to explore, whether it's the mysteries of life or the contents of their own nose. The same impulse that inspires them to experiment and discover also tells them to cut their own hair. It is what has brought us electricity, space exploration, and the vaccine for polio.

It's also what brought us Chernobyl, telemarketing, and the Great Bathroom Flood of 2013.

We want to nurture their exuberant drive, but we also want the species to continue. This is where you come in. If you have a son, you perform heroics every day. You dam geysers, extinguish explosions, patch holes, and bandage boo-boos. You've been mooned and karate-chopped. You have had a child pee in your shoes *while you were wearing them.* You've survived juice stains, waterlogged phones, dropped laptops, and multiple ER visits, and miraculously, the boys have too.

Boys need parents. But the secret truth is that parents need boys. It would be awfully boring without them, wouldn't it?

Still, it might be nice to go one full week without having to call a plumber.

Perhaps he'll be one when he grows up. In the meantime, keep going, have fun, and hope that the grandkids are girls.

To teach him the importance of utensils.

SPOON

NOT A SPOON

Because not everything needs to be a costume.

Because chocolate syrup is not a food group.

Because "snips, snails, and puppy dog tails"
isn't supposed to be taken literally.

Because every superhero
needs a sidekick.

So it won't freeze that way.

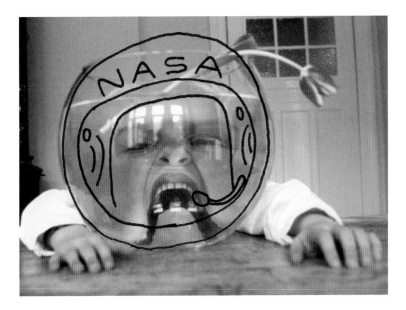

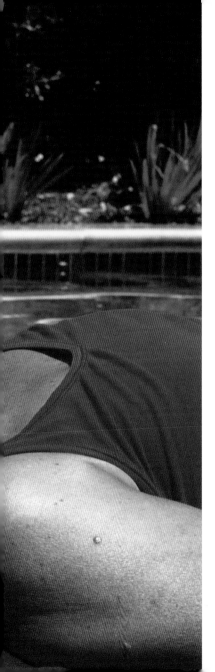

Because Grandma can still change her will.

Because that's not what you meant
by "Clean it inside and out."

Dad will love this!

To help them rethink their priorities.

Because someday, he'll be allowed to drive.

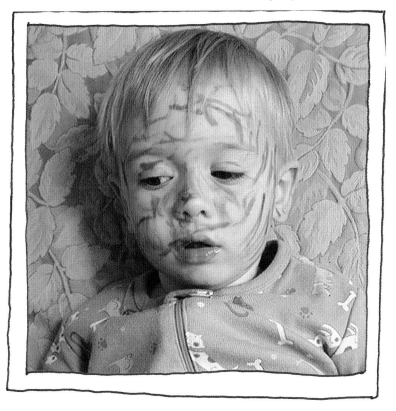

**To explain that a self-portrait is
not a portrait done on one's self.**

What cake?

To keep them honest.

Because we aren't there yet.

To sing back-up.

Because the Creature from the Black Lagoon is not touching the white door with those hands.

Because you can't be leader of the pack
with chocolate sundae on your face.

To referee their cage-match pillow fights.

To check for pool sharks.

To give them a
running start.

This is the good life Mr. Kitty.

Because if it weren't for you, he wouldn't
even be wearing underpants.

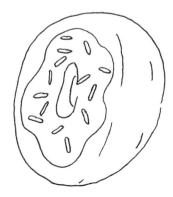

Because Grandma is not King John.

**To explain the difference
between windows and doors.**

Because not everything
needs to be climbed.

**Because every boy needs a
mummy (or daddy).**

For the sake of the person sitting
across the table from him.

**Because they don't always
have an exit strategy.**

Because this happens.

**Because an in-ground pool will
not increase the property value.**

Looking good.

To encourage their fashion sense.

Because they might be organic but
they still don't go in the compost bin.

To foil their jailbreaks.

Because they share their snacks with the
family member that licks its own butt.

Mom says it's good to share.

**Because even the SWAT
team needs backup.**

Because he's not going to nag *himself.*

To conserve our natural resources.

To teach them where the food's supposed to go.

Because it might be hot, and he may
be a dog, but you still cannot eat him.

To water them daily, so they'll grow.

Just one more!

To be their designated driver.

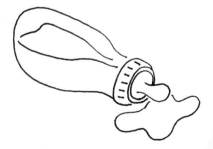

Because where there's smoke, there's a kid playing with illegal fireworks.

I've got to try this indoors.

SUMMER

**Because sand feels better between
your toes than up your nostrils.**

To teach them the art of accessorizing.

**Because they forget
to cut out eyeholes.**

**Because they have the attention
span of—oh look, a squirrel!**

Because sometimes words fail.

Image Credits:

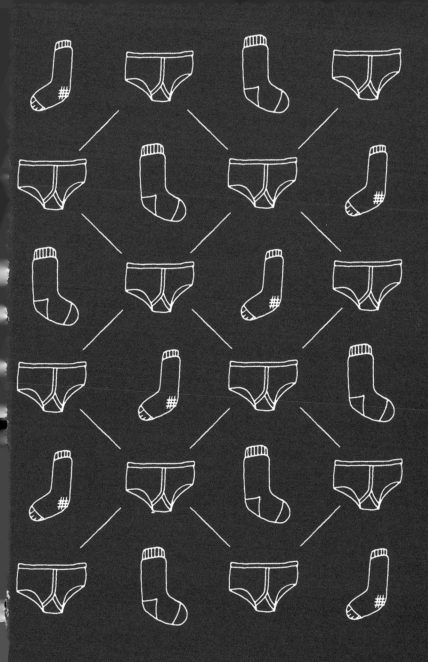

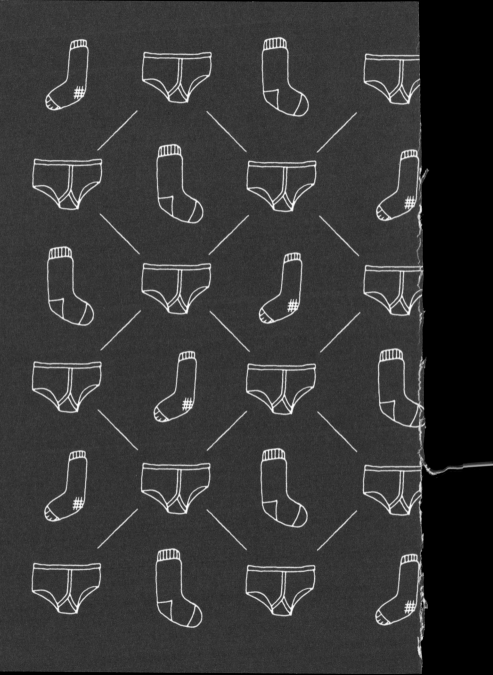